M is for
MINNESOTA

Debra Chial

VOYAGEUR PRESS

ick Minnesota Facts for Kids

ore information about some of the things that Minnesota is famous for. These facts can be read by anced readers (such as parents and older brothers and sisters) to further explain what the Minneso- and symbols mean. A star (*) means this word also appears in the alphabet part of the book.

leaves are beautiful in many parts of the ause of our many *deciduous* trees, or trees their leaves once a year. A forest called *dleaf deciduous forest* grows in much of southeastern, and central Minnesota. es are called *broadleaf* trees because of e leaves, such as maple leaves. *Needleleaf* e narrow leaves, such as **Norway Pine***. he *needleleaf evergreen forest* grows in the northeastern part of the state. *Ever- es* have green leaves all year long.

muffin is the **Blueberry Muffin.**

ndary Waters* Canoe Area Wilderness a's full name) is a favorite canoeing and area for many people. In the BWCAW, you lakes and forests, trails and *portages* follow from one river or lake to another), nd rocks, and animals such as moose, ars, gray wolves, whitetailed deer, and

bird is the **Common Loon,*** but most ay just "loon." Some people call it the orthern Diver."

ople visit **Duluth*** to see the big boats from he world in the Duluth Harbor. Duluth is or an early explorer from France, Daniel n, Sieur du Luth, who came in 1679. Some ay that Du Luth was the first explorer from

that the first people from Europe were the Vikings from Norway in 1362.

Eagle Mountain* is part of the Sawtooth Mountains on the North Shore of Lake Superior. It is 2,301 feet above sea level. It is the highest point in the state.

The **Great Blue Heron*** is the largest heron in Minnesota, and one of the largest birds in the area. Another large bird that lives in Minnesota is the bald eagle.

Our state song is **"Hail! Minnesota."**

Itasca State Park* is the oldest state park in Minnesota. Its "birthday" was in 1891. Today, the park is more than 102 years old.

The **John Beargrease Sled Dog Race*** goes from Duluth to Grand Marais on the North Shore of Lake Superior.

Lake Superior is the largest *freshwater* lake in the world. It is 31,820 square miles in size. *Freshwater* means water that does not have a lot of salt in it, like the ocean has.

Our state rock is the **Lake Superior Agate.** An *agate* can be milky or grayish and can have curved and colored rings.

Minnesota has many more than 10,000 **Lakes.** We

Our largest city is **Minneapolis.**

Almost four and one-half million people live in **Minnesota.**

The name **"Minnesota"*** is taken from a Dakota Indian word meaning "Land of Sky-tinted Waters."

Minnesota* was the thirty-second state to join the United States (in May of 1858).

The **Mississippi River** begins in Minnesota, in **Itasca State Park.*** The beginning of a river is called the *headwaters.* Ojibway Indians led Henry Rowe Schoolcraft to the headwaters in 1832.

Our state motto is "L'Etoile du Nord." This is French, and in English it means **"The North Star."**

Our state nicknames are **"The North Star State," "The Gopher State,"** and **"Land of 10,000 Lakes."**

Minnesota has the northernmost point in the lower forty-eight states. It is the part that looks like a chimney on a map, where **Lake of the Woods** is. This area is called the **Northwest Angle.**

Our state tree is the **Norway Pine,*** which also is called the red pine.

The original people of Minnesota are the **Ojibway*** (also called Anishinabe and Chippewa) and Dakota Indians. From France and other countries came the **Voyageurs,*** people who came to hunt furs and explore the area. Within the last two hundred years, many people came from Germany, Sweden, Norway, and Ireland. They have been followed by people from other continents and countries such as Africa and Russia. Today, we welcome many Hmong *emigrants* (people who have come from another country or region) from Laos.

The statue of **Paul Bunyan and Babe the Blue Ox*** represents the lumber heritage of Minnesota. The first lumber mill in Minnesota was in Marine-on-St. Croix. It was built in 1839 and called "Marine Mills."

Many people are surprised to learn that the **Rivers*** in Minnesota flow in three directions. Some rivers, like the Mississippi and the Minnesota rivers, flow south to the Gulf of Mexico. One of the rivers that flows north to Hudson Bay is the Red River. The Gooseberry River is one river that flows east to Lake Superior.

Our state capital is **St. Paul.**

St. Paul was once named Pig's Eye! Father Lucien Galtier gave the town, which was very small, the new name of St. Paul's Landing, then St. Paul, in the 1840s.

Our state flower is the **Showy Lady's Slipper.** It is a kind of orchid that grows in the *boreal,* or northern, forests.

Our largest lake is actually two lakes on the map, connected in the middle: **Upper and Lower Red Lake** in northern Minnesota.

Our state fish is the **Walleyed Pike.** Sometimes people call this fish "walleye."

Minnesota has fifty-one **Waterfalls.*** The most visited is Gooseberry Falls, on the North Shore of Lake Superior.

The **XY Company*** was formed by voyageurs who worked for the famous North West Company, which had fur posts on the North Shore of Lake Superior.

Aa

is for Autumn leaves, welcomed all across Minnesota in fall.

Bb

is for Boundary Waters, at our border with Canada.

Cc

is for Canoeing on calm waters.

is for Duluth and its delightful lakefront district.

Ee

is for Eagle Mountain and the eagle's-eye view from the highest peak in our state.

is for Fireworks on the Fourth of July and at fun summer festivals.

Gg

is for Great Blue Heron, a grand hero on the water.

is for Hockey, a favorite sport of the north.

Is for Itasca State Park, the source of the Mississippi River, whose name is dotted with "i's."

Jj

is for John Beargrease Sled Dog Race, on the North Shore in January.

Kk

is for a colorful Kayak on Lake Superior.

is for Loon on a Lake and its laughing loon melody.

Mm

is for Minnesota, the thirty-second state.

Nn

is for a Norway Pine in the North Woods, our state tree.

Oo

is for Ojibway, dressed and ready for a powwow.

Pp

is for Paul Bunyan and Babe, his blue ox.

Qq

is for Quilt, to keep quite warm on a quiet Minnesota night.

is for our Rivers, the Rum, Root, Red, Rainy, and more!

Ss

is for
Snow that
we ski on,
sled on,
and
shovel!

Tt

is for Train, like the Minnesota Zephyr, to transport people and things.

Uu

is for
Umbrella
under
rainy
Minnesota
skies.

Vv

is for the brave Voyageurs and their many adventures.

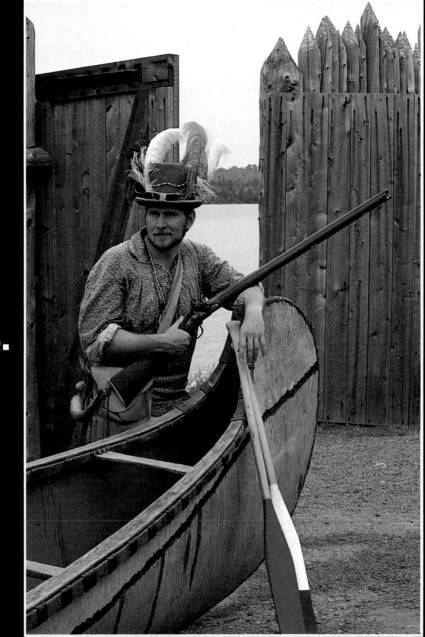

Ww

is for Waterfall, like Gooseberry Falls on the North Shore.

Xx

is for XY Company, trading furs at Grand Portage.

is for "Yah sure, you betcha!," fun to
yell all year long.

is for Zoo, a zany time for everyone.

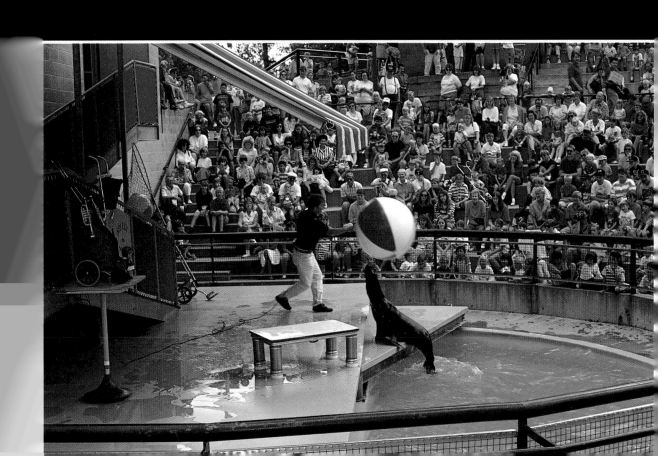

Edited by Helene Anderson and Julie Bach

Printed in Hong Kong
94 95 96 97 98 5 4 3 2 1

Library of Congress Cataloging-in-Publication Data
Chial, Debra, 1964–
        M is for Minnesota / Debra Chial.
        (My State's Alphabet Book series)
                p.   cm.
        ISBN 0-89658-234-5
        1. Minnesota—Juvenile literature. 2. English language—Alphabet—Juvenile literature.
        (1. Minnesota. 2. Alphabet.) I. Title.
        F606.3.C48   1994
        (E)—dc20
        (977.6)   93-34643
                                                                      CIP
                                                                       AC

Published by
VOYAGEUR PRESS, INC.
P.O. Box 338, 123 North Second Street, Stillwater, MN 55082 U.S.A.
612-430-2210

Please write or call, or stop by, for our free catalog of publications. Our TOLL-FREE number to place an order or to obtain a free catalog is 800-888-9653.

Educators, fundraisers, premium and gift buyers, publicists, and marketing managers:
Looking for creative products and new sales ideas? Voyageur Press books are available at special discounts when purchased in quantities, and special editions can be created to your specifications

About the Author

Debra Chial is a lifelong resident of Stillwater, Minnesota. She is a freelance writer and photographer, and recently published her first book, *The St. Croix Valley.* She also has published photos in magazines such as *Minnesota Calls, Minnesota Monthly,* and *Friendly Exchange Magazine,* local newspapers, and publications nationwide. Chial owns a photography and postcard business located in the Old Post Office Shops in downtown Stillwater.

Dedication and Acknowledgments

This book is dedicated to my daughter Melisa, who has enabled me to see through the eyes of a child once again.

I would like to thank the following people for allowing me to take these photos:
C & M: The Williams family at Bear Track Ranch
H: Bob Utecht and grandsons Ben, Joe, and Billy Utecht
K: Stew Joseph
O: Charles Dru
R: Jeff Parker and Melisa Chial
U: Taylor and Ashley Atkins
V: John Sage
X: Natalie Behan and Richard Benning
V & X: Grand Portage monument
Y: Jill and Sarah Clements, Emily and Andrew Stevens, and Melisa Chial
A special thanks to my traveling companions David Chial, Eric Lee, John Herr, Jessie Johnson, and Catie Waisely; and to Marge Wakeling for use of her quilt.